Dissonance.

Rachel Van Gerven

BookLeaf
Publishing

India | USA | UK

Presentation by *BookLeaf Publishing*

Web: www.bookleafpub.com

E-mail: info@bookleafpub.com

ISBN: 978-93-5744-985-4

First edition 2022

DEDICATION

I won't bore you with a sappy dedication, besides who am I dedicating this to? The people who have used and abused me? The narcissist that once had a hold over my life? Actually, I dedicate it to myself and the strength I have built through it all.

Bloodshot

I lay still in the dead of the night
The sound in my ears are static
Growing louder, begins my fight or flight
My chest is tightening and I feel my mind
beginning to waltz
1 2 3, breathe. 1 2 3, breathe.
And when the dancing begins
The war has begun.

Emetophobia

The blacked out moments of being ill
Find the young girl braving a nightmare
Her fragile mind too innocent to understand
She begins to starve.

Daddy! Mummy!
Ouch... my tummy
Please make it stop, I'm scared.
The pain and fear she causes
she's unaware that she has shared.

"Why don't you eat our darling sweet girl?
You need to grow healthy and strong"
Because when I do mummy. my tummy. It
burns.
I can't stand the taste and the pain
Of when it returns.

Red

The colour red was what she saw
Seeping through the torn layers
Of both her mind and her body.
The colour red was what she saw
The build up of tension and rage
It blinds her vision and traps her in a cage.
The colour red is what she saw
As she forced the sweet release
Tearing her skin apart piece by piece.

Ambivalence

Push and pull is the cycle she cannot break
Go ahead leave me
wait no! please stay
I hate you, I hate you.
But please don't walk away.
Love me with all your heart and I will do the
same.
Why don't you just leave then,
if you think I can't be tamed.
My mind is on a rollercoaster and I am ashamed.
I'm sorry I have doubts I just can't bear the pain
Please don't leave me like I leave you
Why can't you understand it's not the same.

Stolen

The room was dimly lit by the crack in the door
It was her comfort from the darkness
that made her feel unsure
That night recalls an unsettling truth
Of the power held over her
in her youth
She began to feel homesick and longed for her
security
A way for her to wash away this impurity
Relief came crashing down like a wave of force
When the crack in the door released more light
to reinforce
A part of her innocence died back then
Never to return to her during her youth again

Changed

Broken down a little at a time
His poisonous venom seeps through to your
heart
Your inner child begins to scream for your help
but she is so distant and apart
The life and love within is left to rot away
at the hands of the serpent that led you astray
You're bound to him with no mercy and
shackled in chains
Helpless to a transition of apathy and cruelty
to no end with your insufferable pain

Unrecognisable

I get high on the fumes of my burning identity
Shedding every layer until I'm left with nothing
but my entity

Stolen from my innocence many moons ago
I keep trying to reach for myself but myself I
don't know

An empty shell of a young girl is all that remains
Stunted and scared
She is unable to express the parts of her she
contains

Switch

Darkness my old friend, will you please come on in
Provide me with the comfort whilst I ride out these sins
The worlds technicolor is draining to grey
I feel the breaking point coming
oh how I wish I could pray
The switch is beginning and the light has died within
My wickedness arises
ready to take its win
Oh the penance I will pay when it's all drawn to a close
No rest for the wicked or those diagnosed

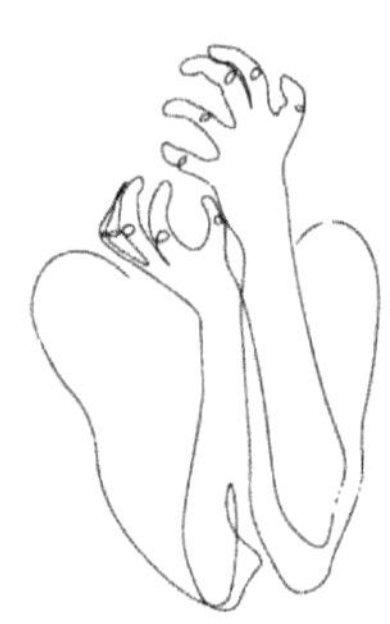

Split

Black and white, yes and no
I'll tell you stay and I'll tell you to go
Emotional impermanence is all that I know
A frightening split and one hell of a show
I'll build you up, to tear you down in slow
Like time has stopped my ability to grow
The mind battles the question, are you friend or fo?
There's no in between in this yes or no
A never ending cycle of reap what I sow

Misguided

We are always told to fear the dark
But little do we know that the darkness lies
within
Playing our hearts' strings like a violin
A gentle melancholy melody
but calmly unnerving
Slowly transforming into something much more
concerning
Our minds begin to dance to the sounds of our
heart
We find comfort in our darkness
With our lightness within, now miles apart
Destruction of each other through a competitive
streak
Is what's on offer for humanity and why we're
so weak.

Impulsion

So blinded by the rush that my soul can't escape
My mind surrenders to its chaotic fate
Scraping at my seams and ready to burst
The impulsiveness succumbs me and my soul is
cursed
No rational thoughts about my consequence
For this gushing creativity is all that I sense
Self destruction is imminent, I take no survivors
Left alone in the darkness once the sun finally
rises

Unapologetic

Battle wounds that will never be repaired
From the destruction to my development they so
openly shared
A life with uncertainty and fear instilled
Through the downplay of emotions that I was
filled
I'm tired. I'm so tired
of living up to your expectations
With no way to navigate through your
impatience
I wasn't given the tools to be able to build
This life you offered me as someone so unskilled
My turbulence disrupts you and you're often
apathetic
But why can't you accept me, is that so pathetic?
Please can't you just be a touch sympathetic?

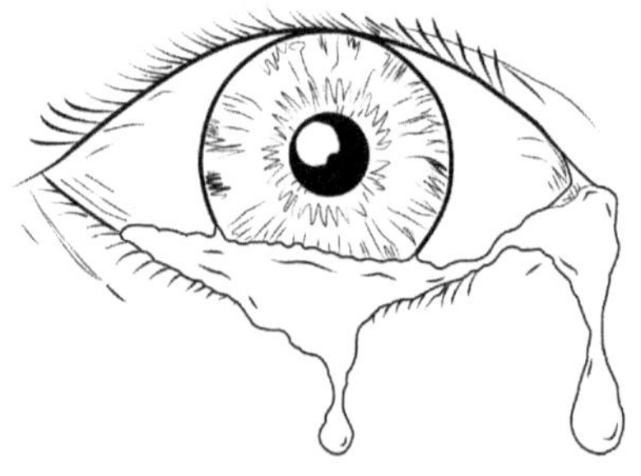

Perception

Was it that she was a drama queen?
Or was it that your level of perception ended
when it came to emotional intensity
Was it that her emotions were exaggerated?
Or was it just your own perplexity
Was it that her moods were rapid?
Or do you just struggle with concept of empathy
Is it just that you don't care to try to understand?
Or is it that you lack the critical thinking skills
to open your mind to see
I don't think it was her all along, I think it was
you and your apathy

Unseen

But did you ever really know me?
Or did you just know the parts of me that were
the mirror I held up to you
Were you ever really in love with me?
Or were you just in love with your self that I
reflected back to you.
Did you ever think to read between the lines?
Or were you so content with how you saw
yourself through my eyes
Did you ever even try to look past this
To realise that maybe just maybe it's you that
you miss?

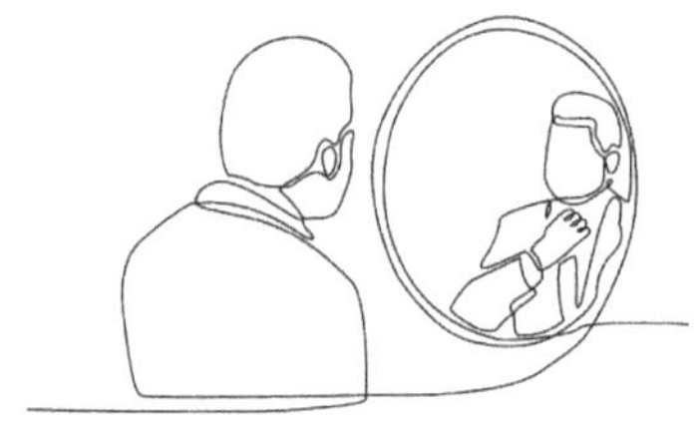

Dissolution

Over time the need to protect you and all that
you were faded
As I began to understand that who you are now
is jaded
Your threats no longer controlled my sympathy
for your condition
As you tried to break me and my love down with
all your ammunition
The ties that bind have snapped for the last time
And I'll no longer allow you to get away with
this crime
You've become what you feared through the
road of resentment and spite
Without trying to look within for answers to heal
and bring back your light
How dare you spew such venomous words to me
And expect I won't react and set a new boundary
Your lack of remorse has left me feeling a lack
of hope
I'm worried about the path you've chosen
but I refuse to stick around for this downward
slope
I hope you find your inner peace and take back
the strength you once had

Don't wind up losing yourself over everything
that has made you mad

Overtaken

Peculiar dreams emerge to reality
In the shadows the figures cry over their
immortality
Unable to move to the skies above
Their souls have been trapped down here
forgotten and unloved
The wind howls at the lonely moon outside
It's pale glow reveals the shadows in sight
You feel your chest clench and tighten you see
The weight crashing down on you from this
large shadowy entity
The darkness washes over you, clouding the
moonlit glow
The world comes to a halt and reality you no
longer know
The heavy pain it has passed on to your soul
Haunted forever by this darkness with no sense
of control

Incorporeal

She was the puzzle piece that never did fit in this place
Fighting to be seen by her peers in this contradictory space
Her jagged edges beginning to fray
In her dreams she would wonder the mystical realms far away
They never really understood her and all the beauty in her chaos
They feared her intensity leaving her wandering this loneliness lost
She fought to tear down the boundaries of her mind
To escape her reality into a new perception of her time
The dreams of enlightenment saw her new path awaiting
A way for her to make sense of herself and what she was creating
Bursting with colours from her sewn together seams
Her lightness now flows outwards in bright colourful beams.

Released

I watched the flames of the two tied candles
engulf the twine
Weakening its link and everything that had
bound us together in our time
The flame on the left rose to a fierce height
Relieving itself of never ending pain and pent up
spite
The right timidly traveling along the rope
Still holding on and still with hope
As they grew closer together the link began to
break
Freedom from one another's connection and
releasing of the heart's ache
The severed twine now dangling side to side
with its permanent disconnection
No way to turn back, only to move forward past
the history of deception

Virulence

I watched him turn on himself to draw them in
Playing on their naivety and need to repair him
from his sin
His silver tongue saturating their minds
And the poison of his soft spoken words
working their crimes
A false sense of control given at the hands of his
vulnerability
A way to ensure his domination over their young
hearts that were once careless and free
He slowly turned on them taking back his power
And held it over them until they slowly became
sour
Their hearts now spoilt and the light in their eyes
dim
Hopelessly digging for their reason to why they
keep disappointing him
Little do they know his misery knows no bounds
He will only continue his consumption of their
love that surrounds

Wuthering

I don't want your lightness and the early
morning sun
How it shines down on our interlocked hearts
and the tracks on my body where your fingers
run
Show me the darkness that lies deep within
The unsettling truths of your mind hidden in the
corners filled with sin
Let's dance on the chaos that runs through our
veins
And enjoy our shadows and the damaged souls
of ours that are trapped in chains
I want to know the parts of you, you never dared
to share with no other
The parts you fear yourself, the ones that make
you shudder
There's beauty in the darkness that they don't
see
It's depth is more than the lightness that they
believe to make them free
We're not like them darling, we're not built to be
pure
We're damaged and in ruin… our love is
obscure

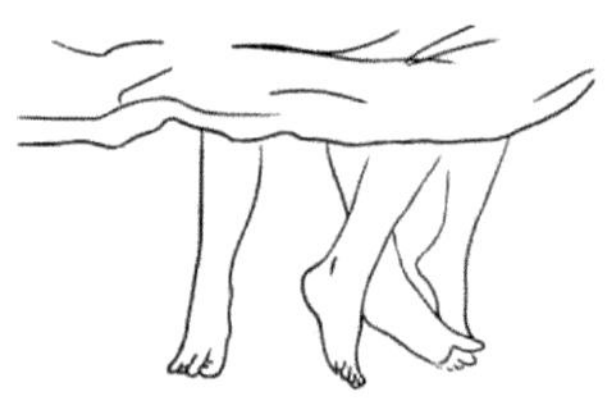

Dolour

I had longed to be swept away by the promises
of most ardently
But was coerced into the realm of the heights in
which had disheartened me
The murdered do haunt their murderers took a
spin you know
Troubled youth sabotage
lovers turned to fo

Incandescently happy
A concept too far of reach
For my troubling mind convinced of me being
left in the abyss
unable to find you
It is unutterable I hiss

Pride and cruelty both on offer for the day
I spare your feelings not
my dear
For you have broken my heart I say

Vengeance was your bliss with the parting of
your mind
I beg you dear
Haunt me

For my life I cannot live
If it is you I cannot find.

www.ingramcontent.com/pod-product-compliance
Lightning Source LLC
LaVergne TN
LVHW051241200726
843510LV00011B/1641